EYE TO EYE WITH DOGS

GOLDEN RETRIEVERS

Lynn M. Stone

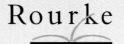

Rourke

Publishing LLC

Vero Beach, Florida 32964

PHOTO CREDITS: All photos © Lynn M. Stone

Cover: *Today's golden retrievers came from a breed begun by Lord Tweedmouth in Scotland in the 1800s.*

Acknowledgments: For their help in the preparation of this book, the author thanks humans June Connelly, Adrian Milbradt, John and Nancy Miner of Miner's Retriever Training (Sheridan, IL), Marsha Schlehr, Brittany Stone, and Shelly Weibel; and canines Bear, Preacher, Rooster, Spirit, Tucker, Zoey, and others.

Editor: Frank Sloan

Cover and page design by Nicola Stratford

Library of Congress Cataloging-in-Publication Data

Stone. Lynn M.
   Golden retrievers / Lynn M. Stone
      p. cm. — (Eye to eye with dogs)
 Summary: A brief introduction to the physical characteristics, temperament, uses, and breeding history of the golden retriever.
  Includes bibliographical references (p.).
  ISBN 1-58952-328-8
  1. Golden retriever—Juvenile literature. [1. Golden retriever. 2. Dogs.] I. Title.

SF429.G63 S76 2002
636.752'7—dc21   2002017837

Printed in the USA

MP/W

Table of Contents

A golden takes time out from a romp with its owner.

The Golden Retriever

Long ago someone said that the dog was "man's best friend." Now, people say, the golden retriever is everyone's best friend! Perhaps no breed of dog shows more **affection** toward people than the handsome, tail-wagging golden.

GOLDEN RETRIEVER FACTS	
Weight:	55-75 pounds (25-34 kilograms)
Height:	21.5-24 inches (54-61 centimeters)
Country of Origin:	Great Britain
Life Span:	12-13 years

Like other retriever breeds, the golden loves to fetch, or retrieve. The love of retrieving is part of the golden's **instinct**.

Bird down! A golden streaks across corn stubble to retrieve a pheasant.

Goldens are gentle pets, which is one reason for their popularity.

Goldens are one of the so-called sporting, or gundog, breeds. Goldens are trained by hunters to retrieve ducks, geese, and other game birds. Goldens are also one of the three breeds commonly used as guide, or seeing-eye, dogs.

Popular and Friendly Dogs

The great majority of golden retrievers are not working dogs, however. Rather, they are household companions. Their friendly nature makes them especially popular in homes with small children.

In recent years goldens have been the second most popular **purebred** dog in North America. In both the United States and Canada, new **registrations** for goldens trail only those of Labrador retrievers.

Lovable goldens rank as the second most popular purebred dog in North America.

Old-time retrievers of England had flat coats, much like this Chesapeake retriever's.

Goldens of the Past

Lord Tweedmouth was a wealthy Scotsman. He loved hunting and he loved hunting dogs. The common retrievers of Tweedmouth's day had dark, flat coats. Tweedmouth wanted a handsome retriever with a longhaired, yellow coat.

In 1868 Tweedmouth **mated** a male yellow retriever with a female Tweed water spaniel. Their four pups weren't golden retrievers. They were, however, the beginning of the breed.

Over the next several years, Tweedmouth used the grown pups and several other dogs as parents. He used red setters, a bloodhound, and more retrievers and Tweed water spaniels. (The Tweed water spaniel is now **extinct**.)

Lord Tweedmouth wanted a handsome, new retrieving breed with a long, yellow coat.

Lord Tweedmouth's new breed proved to be at home in snow as well as in water.

Many people considered Tweedmouth's dogs just a yellow variety of the flat-coated retriever. But in 1912, The Kennel Club of England recognized the golden retriever as a breed.

Lord Tweedmouth's sons had brought goldens to America by 1900. Still, the American Kennel Club (AKC) did not accept goldens as a separate breed until 1927.

State of the art: a model golden retriever

Yellow as the corn stubble around it, a golden retriever waits for a command.

Looks

Goldens have fine, athletic builds similar to those of other retrievers. A **well-bred** golden has a broad head with wide, floppy ears and a fairly square **muzzle**.

Long hair helps separate goldens from yellow Labrador retrievers. Goldens wear a fringe of hair called "feathers" along their legs, underside, and tail.

The coats of golden retrievers range from red-gold to nearly white. A dense undercoat lies beneath the long outer coat.

Golden Companions

Almost always good-natured, goldens demand human attention. A golden retriever begins wagging its tail each time a stranger appears. A golden seems to welcome everyone as a new friend.

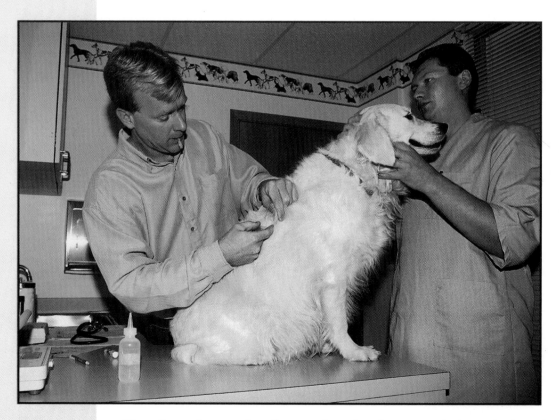

Regular trips to the doctor for checkups and shots help keep this female golden a healthy companion.

Being a good human companion means keeping your longhaired golden well groomed.

Generally, adult goldens are calm, relaxed dogs that bark little. But they are athletic dogs with plenty of energy. They love to swim, run, romp, play fetch, and sniff about the woods.

Goldens are eager, easy learners. They love to please their human masters. They do very well in **obedience** tests where they follow a variety of commands.

Each breed of dog has certain "standards." Standards include such things as proper height, weight, color, and shape. Many goldens are entered in shows that judge how closely they meet the breed standards.

An athletic, airborne golden retriever leaps over a jumping bar.

A Note About Dogs

Puppies are cute and cuddly, but buying one should never be done without serious thought. Choosing the right breed of dog requires some homework. And remember that a dog will require more than love and great patience. It will require food, exercise, grooming, a warm, safe place to live, and medical care.

A dog can be your best friend, but you need to be its best friend, too. For more information about buying and owning a dog, contact the American Kennel Club at http://www.akc.org/index.cfm or the Canadian Kennel Club at http://www.ckc.ca/.

Glossary

affection (uh FEK shun) — friendliness toward another creature

extinct (iks TINKT) — to have gone out of existence

instinct (IN stinkt) — action or behavior with which an animal is born, rather than learned behavior

mated (MAY tud) — to have been paired with another dog for the purpose of having pups

muzzle (MUZ uhl) — the nose and jaws of an animal; the snout

obedience (oh BEE dee ehns) — the willingness to follow someone's direction or command

purebred (PYOOR bred) — an animal of a single (pure) breed

registrations (rehj uh STRAY shunz) — official records of membership in a group

well-bred (WEL BRED) — to have come from outstanding ancestors and parents

Index

Further Reading

Huxley, Joanne P. *The Guide to Owning a Golden Retriever*. Chelsea House, 1999

Wilcox, Charlotte. *The Golden Retriever*. Capstone Press, 1996

Websites to Visit

http://www.golden-retriever.com/golden.html
Golden Retriever Club of America at http://www.grca.org
Working Retriever Central at http://working-retriever.com/

About the Author

Lynn Stone is the author of over 400 children's books. He is a talented natural history photographer as well. Lynn, a former teacher, travels worldwide to photograph wildlife in its natural habitat.